VALLEY 1/
5069001078
Jasner, Andy,
Baltimore Ravens /

VALLEY COMMUNITY LIBRARY
739 RIVER STREET
PECKVILLE, PA 18452
(570) 489-1765
www.lclshome.org

BALTIMORE RAVENS

by Andy Jasner

Published by ABDO Publishing Company, 8000 West 78th Street, Edina, Minnesota 55439. Copyright © 2011 by Abdo Consulting Group, Inc. International copyrights reserved in all countries. No part of this book may be reproduced in any form without written permission from the publisher. SportsZone™ is a trademark and logo of ABDO Publishing Company.

Printed in the United States of America,
North Mankato, Minnesota
062010
092010

 THIS BOOK CONTAINS AT LEAST 10% RECYCLED MATERIALS.

Editor: Matt Tustison
Copy Editor: Nicholas Cafarelli
Interior Design and Production: Craig Hinton
Cover Design: Kazuko Collins

Photo Credits: Winslow Townson/AP Images, cover; Nick Wass/AP Images, title page; Tony Gutierrez/AP Images, 4; Chuck Burton/AP Images, 7; David Phillip/AP Images, 8, 42 (middle); Rick Bowmer/AP Images, 11, 43 (top); Wally Santana/AP Images, 12; Bill Smith/AP Images, 15; Ted Mathias/AP Images, 16, 42 (top); John Dunn/AP Images, 18; AP Images, 21; Bill Kostroun/AP Images, 23; John Russell/AP Images, 24, 42 (bottom); Rusty Kennedy/AP Images, 26; Gail Burton/AP Images, 29, 32; Nick Wass/AP Images, 31; Orlin Wagner/AP Images, 34; Rusty Kennedy/AP Images, 36, 43 (middle); Rob Carr/AP Images, 39; Elise Amendola/AP Images, 41, 43 (bottom); David Stluka/AP Images, 44; Julia Robertson/AP Images, 47

Library of Congress Cataloging-in-Publication Data
Jasner, Andy, 1969-
  Baltimore Ravens / Andy Jasner.
    p. cm. — (Inside the NFL)
  ISBN 978-1-61714-003-7
  1. Baltimore Ravens (Football team)—History—Juvenile literature. I. Title.
  GV956.B3J37 2010
  796.332'64097526—dc22
                                        2010018840

TABLE OF CONTENTS

Chapter 1 .... Greatest Defense Ever? 4

Chapter 2 .... Baltimore's Second Chance, 12

Chapter 3 .... The Early Seasons, 18

Chapter 4 .... Trying to Recapture Glory, 26

Chapter 5 .... Return to Winning Ways, 34

Timeline, 42

Quick Stats, 44

Quotes and Anecdotes, 45

Glossary, 46

For More Information, 47

Index, 48

About the Author, 48

CHAPTER 1

GREATEST DEFENSE EVER?

Which National Football League (NFL) team had the best defense of all time? It is a question that many football fans have debated. Some legendary teams are mentioned often when the topic comes up. Among them are the 2000 Baltimore Ravens.

In 2000, the Ravens featured a rugged, swarming defense that led the team all the way to a Super Bowl title. In the regular season, the Ravens set NFL records for fewest points (165) and rushing yards (970) allowed in a 16-game schedule. Baltimore shut out four opponents. The Ravens did not have the most talented offense. But on the strength of the team's defense, Baltimore finished 12–4 and earned a wild-card playoff berth.

In the postseason, the Ravens' defense played even better. Baltimore was stingy in allowing other teams to score. The Ravens defeated the visiting Denver Broncos 21–3 and the

LINEBACKER JAMIE SHARPER CELEBRATES HIS INTERCEPTION IN THE RAVENS' 34–7 WIN OVER THE GIANTS IN SUPER BOWL XXXV ON JANUARY 28, 2001.

GREATEST DEFENSE EVER?

host Tennessee Titans 24–10. In the American Football Conference (AFC) Championship Game against the Oakland Raiders, the Ravens forced five turnovers. Baltimore also held Oakland to 24 rushing yards on 17 carries. The Ravens won 16–3.

A 96-yard touchdown pass in the second quarter from Trent Dilfer to tight end Shannon Sharpe was all the offense the Ravens needed against the Raiders.

"We've got one more challenge," Baltimore defensive coordinator Marvin Lewis said of his defense afterward, referring to the Super Bowl. "They want to make their mark in history."

Ray Lewis, who was named the 2000 NFL Defensive Player of the Year, led the Ravens' defense. Peter Boulware and Jamie Sharper formed a standout linebacker trio with Lewis. Sam Adams and Tony Siragusa were excellent run stoppers at the tackle positions. Ends Rob Burnett and Michael McCrary could put pressure on quarterbacks. Then there was the secondary, led by future Hall of Famer Rod Woodson at safety. Kim Herring

THE "D" DEBATE

What are some of the other teams that are brought up frequently when football fans discuss which squad had the greatest defense in NFL history? The 1985 Chicago Bears, led by standouts such as linebacker Mike Singletary, went 15–1 and won a Super Bowl crown with a tough-as-nails defense. In the 1970s, the Pittsburgh Steelers' defense was known as the "Steel Curtain." The defense included Hall of Fame players such as defensive tackle "Mean" Joe Greene. Four Steelers teams from the 1970s won Super Bowls. In the 1970s, the Minnesota Vikings' "Purple People Eaters" defense featured multiple Hall of Famers. The 1986 and 1990 New York Giants won Super Bowls with the help of stout defenses. Hall of Fame linebacker Lawrence Taylor was the star. The 2000 Ravens, in terms of statistics, compare well with all those teams.

LINEBACKER RAY LEWIS, SHOWN DURING A PLAYOFF GAME AGAINST THE TITANS IN JANUARY 2001, WAS THE LEADER OF THE RAVENS' SUPERB DEFENSE.

was the other safety. Chris McAlister and Duane Starks were the cornerbacks who could shut down opponents' wide receivers.

Baltimore's offense was not flashy. But it played well enough to help the team win. Dilfer, a veteran, replaced Tony Banks as the starting quarterback partway through the season and finished with 12 touchdown passes against 11 interceptions.

BRIAN BILLICK

The 2000 Ravens were coached by Brian Billick. Billick was hired as coach before the 1999 season. He previously was the offensive coordinator for the Minnesota Vikings from 1992 to 1998. In 1998, the Vikings scored a record 556 points under Billick's guidance. With the Ravens, he found himself with a team known for defense. He proved that he could change his coaching style. The Vikings threw the ball often under Billick. But the Ravens' offense tried to use up time on the clock by running frequently. This allowed the defense to be well rested and dominate.

THE RAVENS' TRENT DILFER PREPARES TO LET GO OF A PASS DURING SUPER BOWL XXXV. DILFER FINISHED 12-FOR-25 FOR 153 YARDS AND A TOUCHDOWN.

Rookie running back Jamal Lewis rushed for 1,364 yards. Sharpe was the team's top pass catcher with 67 receptions. Wide receiver Qadry Ismail gave the passing attack a deep threat.

On special teams, the Ravens had standout players in speedy return man Jermaine Lewis and reliable kicker Matt Stover.

But it was defense for which the 2000 Ravens were known. The defense would have a chance to demonstrate to the world just how good it was when Baltimore faced the New York Giants in Super Bowl XXXV on

January 28, 2001. The game was held at Raymond James Stadium in Tampa, Florida.

The Super Bowl turned into a showcase for the Ravens' defense. Baltimore allowed just 152 yards, forced five turnovers, recorded four sacks, and did not give up an offensive touchdown in a 34–7 win. The Ravens forced the Giants' Kerry Collins into 15-for-39 passing for just 112 yards with four interceptions.

Dilfer's 38-yard touchdown pass to Brandon Stokley in the first quarter and Stover's 47-yard field goal in the second staked the Ravens to a 10–0 lead at halftime. Then, in the third quarter, Starks intercepted a pass by Collins and returned it 49 yards for a touchdown, giving the Ravens a 17–0 lead.

The only scare for Baltimore in the second half came when Ron Dixon's 97-yard kickoff return for a touchdown cut the Ravens' lead to 17–7. But Baltimore responded to that immediately with Jermaine Lewis's 84-yard kickoff return for a touchdown that put Baltimore ahead 24–7. In the fourth quarter, Jamal Lewis ran for a 3-yard touchdown and Stover made a 34-yard field goal. The Giants gained just one first down on their final four possessions.

TRENT DILFER

Trent Dilfer was the Ravens' starting quarterback for much of their championship run in the 2000 regular season and postseason. Dilfer had played his first six NFL seasons with Tampa Bay. The Buccaneers released him in February 2000. The Ravens signed Dilfer the next month to serve as the backup quarterback to Tony Banks. Banks struggled early in the 2000 season. Dilfer took over as the starter. The Ravens lost the first game that he started but won the final 11, counting the playoffs. After the 2000 season, the Ravens let Dilfer go. But his one year with Baltimore was a huge success.

GREATEST DEFENSE EVER?

BETTER TIMES FOR LEWIS

Linebacker Ray Lewis might have been happier about the Ravens' Super Bowl win than anyone. "I had a higher power that said everything's going to be all right," he said.

About a year earlier—on January 31, 2000, the day after Super Bowl XXXIV, in Atlanta, Georgia—Lewis was at the scene of a fight that resulted in the stabbing deaths of Jacinth Baker and Richard Lollar. Lewis and two companions, Reginald Oakley and Joseph Sweeting, were indicted on murder and aggravated assault charges.

Lewis's lawyer arranged for the murder charges against him to be dropped in exchange for testimony against Oakley and Sweeting. Lewis pleaded guilty to a lesser charge of obstruction of justice. He was sentenced to one year of probation. The NFL fined him $250,000. Oakley and Sweeting were acquitted of the charges in June 2000.

Dilfer threw no interceptions. Jamal Lewis ran for 102 yards on 27 carries. Again, the Ravens got the job done with an efficient performance from the offense and a dominant effort from the defense.

Ray Lewis was named the Super Bowl Most Valuable Player (MVP). The heart and soul of the Ravens' defense finished with 11 tackles and six assists.

"Our defense has been doing this all year," the linebacker said. "No one can ever take this away from us. We're the best ever."

On January 30, 2001, the Ravens held a victory parade through downtown Baltimore. Rain and cold weather did not stop more than 200,000 people from packing the streets and celebrating the team's

RAY LEWIS SMILES AFTER THE RAVENS ROUTED THE GIANTS IN THE SUPER BOWL. "WE'VE DOMINATED PEOPLE LIKE THAT ALL YEAR," HE SAID.

Super Bowl title. Players spoke to the adoring fans.

The 2000 season was a magical ride for the Ravens. Making it even more special for fans in Baltimore was that the team was in just its fifth season of existence. Baltimore was no stranger to the NFL, though. The city had been home to an NFL team before, the Baltimore Colts, only to see it leave. With the Ravens, "Charm City," as Baltimore is known, was thrilled to have a championship franchise again.

CHAPTER 2
BALTIMORE'S SECOND CHANCE

Long before the Ravens ever played in Baltimore, the Maryland city had another NFL team: the Colts. The Colts were one of the most storied teams in the league. They won NFL titles. They had legendary players such as quarterback Johnny Unitas.

In 1984, though, the Colts' owner decided to move the team to Indianapolis, Indiana. Fans in Baltimore were heartbroken when the Colts secretly moved away in the wee hours of a snowy morning on March 29. The entire team and its belongings were packed up on moving trucks and headed for Indianapolis.

Just like that, the Colts' time was over in Baltimore.

From the early 1950s to the early 1980s, the Baltimore Colts were one of the NFL's most highly regarded teams. They won NFL championships in 1958, 1959, and 1968 and a Super Bowl title after the 1970 season.

OFFENSIVE TACKLE JONATHAN OGDEN, SHOWN WITH NFL COMMISSIONER PAUL TAGLIABUE IN APRIL 1996, WAS THE RAVENS' FIRST DRAFT PICK EVER.

> **JOHNNY UNITAS**
>
> In 1956, the Baltimore Colts signed quarterback Johnny Unitas for a reported $17,000. Unitas, a former University of Louisville standout, was taken in the ninth round of the NFL Draft in 1955 by his hometown Pittsburgh Steelers. The team released him, however. Unitas would go on to play with the Colts and become a record-setting quarterback. In December 1958, Unitas guided the Colts past the host New York Giants 23–17 in overtime for the NFL title in "The Greatest Game Ever Played." Unitas led the Colts to another NFL Championship Game win in 1959. Unitas played with Baltimore until 1972. He passed away in 2002. There is a statue of him outside M&T Bank Stadium—the Ravens' home.

So when owner Robert Irsay decided to move the Colts, he was taking a lot of history with him. Baltimoreans were angry. Eventually, though, they focused on getting another NFL team.

In the 1990s, Baltimore was one of the five finalists for two NFL expansion franchises. Charlotte, North Carolina (the Carolina Panthers), and Jacksonville, Florida (the Jacksonville Jaguars), had the winning bids, though.

Another opportunity for Baltimore to land an NFL team developed in 1995. Cleveland Browns owner Art Modell was not happy with the condition of his team's Municipal Stadium. Late that year, Modell revealed that he was moving the tradition-rich Browns from Cleveland to Baltimore, where a new stadium would be built. It was similar to how the Colts left Baltimore.

The city of Cleveland made legal efforts to prevent the Browns from leaving. Eventually, a settlement was reached in which Cleveland would get an NFL expansion team in 1999. That team would be called the Browns and be considered the same franchise as the old Browns franchise. The team that moved

BALTIMORE COLTS OWNER ROBERT IRSAY GETS INTO A SHOUTING MATCH WITH REPORTERS IN JANUARY 1984. HE DENIED THAT HE WAS MOVING THE TEAM. TWO MONTHS LATER, THE COLTS LEFT FOR INDIANAPOLIS.

to Baltimore in 1996 would get a different name and be thought of as a new franchise. But it would inherit the Browns' players.

The fans in Baltimore were thrilled. They would have an NFL team again.

The Browns relocated to Baltimore in early 1996. Bill Belichick had stepped down as the team's coach after the 1995 season. In need of a replacement,

IRSAY'S DECISION

Colts owner Robert Irsay had wanted the Maryland state legislature to help pay for improvements to aging Memorial Stadium in Baltimore for years. When the legislature stalled, he began entertaining the thought of moving the Colts. On March 27, 1984, the Maryland Senate passed legislation that would give the city of Baltimore the right to take over ownership of the team. This worried Irsay. As a result, he quickly accepted an offer from Indianapolis to move the Colts to that city. Indianapolis' Hoosier Dome was set to open. That is where the Colts ended up playing in 1984 and for several years afterward.

ART MODELL, *LEFT*, AND BALTIMORE MAYOR KURT SCHMOKE SHARE A LAUGH DURING A NEWS CONFERENCE IN NOVEMBER 1995. MODELL ANNOUNCED THAT HE WAS MOVING THE CLEVELAND BROWNS TO BALTIMORE.

Modell hired Ted Marchibroda. Marchibroda had coached the Baltimore Colts from 1975 to 1979 and the Indianapolis Colts from 1992 to 1995. He led the Colts to the AFC title game after the 1995 season. Modell also brought former Browns star tight end Ozzie Newsome, who worked in Cleveland's front office, to Baltimore. Newsome would be the vice president of pro personnel.

Now the new Baltimore team needed a name. The franchise had the *Baltimore Sun* newspaper conduct a telephone poll. There were three nickname finalists: Ravens, Americans, and Marauders. Ravens received the most votes by far. On March 29, 1996, the team was officially named the Ravens. The name was selected in honor of Edgar Allan Poe. He penned his famous poem "The Raven" while living in Baltimore. Team colors of purple, black, gold, and white were selected.

The next step was the team's first NFL Draft, on April 20. With their first two picks, the Ravens chose offensive tackle Jonathan Ogden (fourth overall) and linebacker Ray Lewis (twenty-sixth overall). Both would become Hall of Fame-caliber players.

The Browns team that Baltimore was receiving had not enjoyed much success in the seasons before the move. But fans in Baltimore were willing to give the team time. It was now their team, the Ravens. They were embracing the return of the NFL.

BALTIMORE'S CFL TEAM

In 1994 and 1995, Baltimore had a team in the Canadian Football League. Home games were held at Memorial Stadium. This demonstrated how hungry the city's fans were to see professional football.

The CFL had started admitting U.S. teams in 1993. The Baltimore team began play in 1994 as a new squad. The team was originally called the Colts. But the NFL filed a lawsuit. The CFL team backed off. Baltimore's CFL team went without a nickname for the 1994 season. Instead, it was called the Baltimore Football Club. The team became known as the Stallions before the 1995 season. That year, the team won the Grey Cup.

The Stallions would move to Montreal for the 1996 season. However, Baltimore's brief time in the CFL was rewarding. The CFL team's fan support helped convince Art Modell to make the decision to move the Browns to Baltimore.

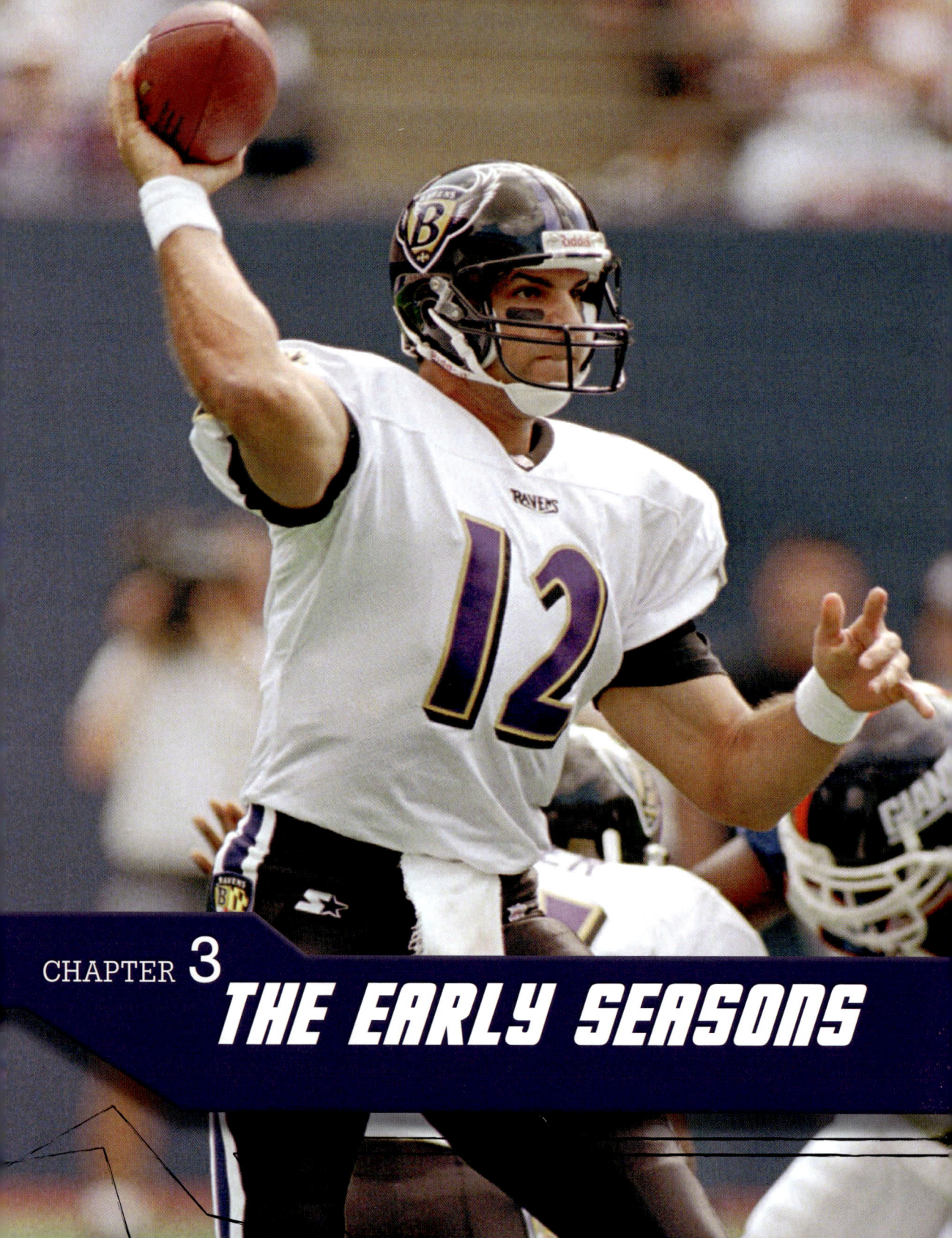

CHAPTER 3
THE EARLY SEASONS

The Ravens' first few seasons featured little on-field success. The Cleveland Browns had struggled in the seasons before the team moved to Baltimore in 1996. It would take time for the Ravens to build a winner.

Still, fans in Baltimore were pumped up for the 1996 season opener on September 1 at Memorial Stadium. It was the same stadium that the Baltimore Colts had played in. The Ravens would need to play at Memorial Stadium until a new football venue could be built in the city.

The Ravens won that first game, beating the Oakland Raiders 19–14 in front of 64,124 fans. Quarterback Vinny Testaverde scored the game's first touchdown on a 9-yard run. Matt Stover made two field goals. Earnest Byner's 1-yard touchdown run in the fourth quarter was the decisive score.

The rest of the season would not go as well for the Ravens. The team was competitive in many

NFL VETERAN VINNY TESTAVERDE WAS THE RAVENS' STARTING QUARTERBACK THEIR FIRST TWO YEARS, IN 1996 AND 1997.

VINNY TESTAVERDE

Vinny Testaverde had already played nine seasons in the NFL when the Ravens made their debut in 1996. Testaverde won the Heisman Trophy in 1986 while playing at the University of Miami in Florida. Tampa Bay selected him with the first overall pick in the 1987 NFL Draft. He mostly struggled during six seasons with the Buccaneers. He then signed with Cleveland and improved. Testaverde made the move with the Browns to Baltimore in 1996. He excelled during the Ravens' first year. He enjoyed one of his finest seasons in the NFL with 4,177 yards and 33 touchdowns passing. He would play one more season with the Ravens and then sign with the New York Jets. He helped the 1998 Jets advance to the AFC title game. Testaverde continued to play in the NFL until 2007, when he was 44 years old.

games but went 4–12. Baltimore finished in last place in the AFC Central Division. The Ravens' fellow teams in the AFC Central were the Cincinnati Bengals, Houston Oilers, Jacksonville Jaguars, and Pittsburgh Steelers.

Testaverde's play was a pleasant surprise in 1996. The veteran had his best season in the NFL to that point. He threw for 4,177 yards and 33 touchdowns against 19 interceptions. He was selected to the Pro Bowl. Wide receivers Michael Jackson (76 catches for 1,201 yards) and Derrick Alexander (62 catches for 1,099 yards) were key factors in the passing attack. The team's defense struggled, however.

The Ravens got off to a solid start in 1997, winning three of their first four games. Baltimore then only won one of the next nine games. A 10–10 tie with the Philadelphia Eagles was included in that stretch. The Ravens finished 6–9–1 and again in last place in the AFC Central.

The Ravens defeated the Tennessee Oilers (the team had relocated from Houston) 21–19 in their final game at Memorial Stadium on December 14, 1997. Past players in Baltimore's

FANS ARRIVE AT THE NEW RAVENS STADIUM FOR BALTIMORE'S FIRST GAME THERE, AN EXHIBITION CONTEST IN AUGUST 1998 AGAINST THE CHICAGO BEARS.

professional football history were honored that day. Another highlight of the 1997 season was the play of rookie linebacker Peter Boulware. Boulware finished with 11.5 sacks and was selected as the NFL Defensive Rookie of the Year. Linebacker Ray Lewis was also sensational with 156 solo tackles. He was selected to his first Pro Bowl.

On September 6, 1998, the Ravens made their regular-season debut in their new home, Ravens Stadium at Camden Yards. Baltimore fell 20–13 to Pittsburgh.

NO PLACE LIKE HOME

On September 6, 1998, the Ravens opened the season with a game against the Pittsburgh Steelers. The contest was the first at the Ravens' sparkling new stadium, then called Ravens Stadium at Camden Yards.

Ground was broken for the football-only facility in mid-1996. The stadium was built downtown, adjacent to Oriole Park at Camden Yards—the home of the Baltimore Orioles baseball team. Ravens Stadium was constructed to seat about 70,000 people. It cost an estimated $220 million and was paid for by a combination of public and team funds.

The stadium became known as PSINet Stadium in 1999 when that company bought the naming rights. It went back to Ravens Stadium in 2002, then became M&T Bank Stadium in 2003. The stadium originally had a natural-grass playing surface. In 2003, artificial turf was installed.

The rest of the season was pretty unspectacular for the Ravens. An exception was the team's game on November 29 against the Indianapolis Colts. It was the Colts' first contest in Baltimore since 1983. The Ravens rallied for 25 points in the second half to pull out a 38–31 win over the Colts and rookie quarterback Peyton Manning. The Baltimore fans loved it. Jim Harbaugh passed for two touchdowns for the Ravens.

Baltimore finished 1998 with a 6–10 record and in fourth place. Harbaugh, an NFL veteran, had been acquired before the season from Indianapolis. Testaverde, the Ravens' starting quarterback their first two seasons, signed with the New York Jets before the 1998 season. The Ravens had trouble on offense that season. The defense added a key player when future

ROD WOODSON RETURNS AN INTERCEPTION AGAINST THE JETS IN 1998. THE DEFENSIVE BACK WAS A KEY PART OF THE RAVENS' DEFENSE FROM 1998 TO 2001.

Hall of Fame defensive back Rod Woodson signed with the team before the season began. Woodson had been let go by the San Francisco 49ers.

Baltimore decided not to renew Ted Marchibroda's contract after the 1998 season. He finished with a 16–31–1 record in three years as the Ravens' coach. Baltimore hired former Minnesota offensive coordinator Brian Billick as his replacement. Billick had helped guide the

MANY HAPPY RETURNS

On December 13, 1998, the Ravens and visiting Vikings set an NFL record when they combined for three kickoff returns for touchdowns. All of them happened in the first quarter. Corey Harris (95 yards) and Patrick Johnson (97 yards) scored for Baltimore. David Palmer (88 yards) reached the end zone for Minnesota. The Ravens lost the game 38–28.

THE EARLY SEASONS

RAVENS COACH BRIAN BILLICK AND PLAYERS CELEBRATE DURING THE TEAM'S 24–23 ROAD WIN OVER THE TITANS IN NOVEMBER 2000.

Vikings' record-setting offense in 1998.

The Ravens acquired promising young quarterback Tony Banks from the St. Louis Rams before the 1999 season. He would be Baltimore's starter. Harbaugh signed with the San Diego Chargers.

Baltimore got off to another slow start in 1999, losing five of its first seven games. Then the team got hot toward the end of the season. The Ravens were 8–7 going into the final week. They had a chance to make the playoffs. Baltimore fell 20–3 to the host New England Patriots, however. The Ravens finished in third place in the AFC Central.

Baltimore saw improvement on offense in 1999. Newcomers Banks and wide receiver

Qadry Ismail (68 catches for 1,105 yards), a former Viking, helped lead the way. But the most noticeable change was that the defense had become excellent. It ranked sixth in the NFL in points allowed and second in yards allowed. It was led by Lewis (131 solo tackles, three interceptions), Woodson (seven interceptions), and Boulware (10 sacks). Rookie Chris McAlister was an immediate standout, recording five interceptions. Defensive end Michael McCrary had 11.5 sacks.

The Ravens' success at the end of 1999 carried over into the 2000 season. The defense got even better. The team added Sam Adams, formerly of the Seattle Seahawks, to pair with Tony Siragusa as a run-stuffing defensive tackle duo. Baltimore selected running back Jamal Lewis with its first pick in the draft. He became a major contributor right away. The Ravens also signed veteran quarterback Trent Dilfer. He would prove to be a perfect fit for the team. It all added up to a Super Bowl title and the most memorable season in team history.

Living up to the 2000 season was perhaps an impossible task. The Ravens would discover that the rest of the decade. But the defense, led by Lewis, would continue to be very impressive.

> **TONY BANKS**
>
> Tony Banks was 6–4 as a starting quarterback for the Ravens in 1999. He threw a career-best 17 touchdown passes with just eight interceptions. The stingy Ravens defense would get most of the accolades. But Banks played well. He was a Raven for one more season. Overall, he played nine seasons in the NFL and threw for 77 touchdowns against 73 interceptions.

CHAPTER 4

TRYING TO RECAPTURE GLORY

The Ravens had a lot to live up to after their Super Bowl-winning season in 2000. Many football followers considered that squad's defense to be among the best in NFL history. The defense would remain strong in 2001. But the team made a switch at quarterback that had many people scratching their heads.

Baltimore released Trent Dilfer before the 2001 season. Some in the Ravens organization felt that the team had won the Super Bowl mainly because of its defense and running game.

Dilfer ended up signing with Seattle to be a backup to starter Matt Hasselbeck. Dilfer would play well in six games for the Seahawks in 2001. But for the rest of his NFL career, which ended after the 2007 season, Dilfer would not regain the stature he had with Baltimore in 2000.

The Ravens, meanwhile, signed Elvis Grbac to a five-year contract to be the team's new

QUARTERBACK ELVIS GRBAC LOOKS ON FROM THE SIDELINE DURING THE RAVENS' 27–10 PLAYOFF LOSS TO THE STEELERS IN JANUARY 2002.

TRYING TO RECAPTURE GLORY   27

> ## OZZIE NEWSOME
>
> When the Ravens promoted vice president of pro personnel Ozzie Newsome to general manager (GM) in November 2002, he became the first minority GM in NFL history. Newsome had earned a reputation as a top-notch talent evaluator. The Ravens drafted standouts such as linebacker Ray Lewis, offensive tackle Jonathan Ogden, linebacker Peter Boulware, cornerback Chris McAlister, running back Jamal Lewis, and safety Ed Reed under Newsome's guidance before his promotion. He continued an excellent track record in evaluating talent, in the NFL Draft and in the free-agent pool, after he became GM.

starting quarterback. Grbac was coming off a Pro Bowl season in 2000 with the Kansas City Chiefs. Still, it bothered many Ravens players and fans that Dilfer was let go by the team.

The Ravens' attempt to defend their title took a huge blow before the 2001 season even started. Standout running back Jamal Lewis suffered a season-ending knee injury in training camp. Despite this, Baltimore started 6–3. The defense led the way. The team's chemistry was off, however. Some players criticized Grbac in the press. The Ravens finished 10–6 and sneaked into the playoffs as a wild card. Baltimore beat the host Miami Dolphins 20–3 in the first round but then fell 27–10 at Pittsburgh in the divisional round. Grbac threw three interceptions against the Steelers. The Ravens released Grbac following the season. He ended up retiring from the NFL.

In 2002, Baltimore could not keep all of its talented players because doing so would make the team's payroll too high for NFL rules. On defense, secondary players Rod Woodson and Duane Starks, end Rob Burnett, and tackle Sam Adams signed with other teams. On offense, star tight end Shannon Sharpe

RAVENS OWNER ART MODELL, *LEFT*, AND GENERAL MANAGER OZZIE NEWSOME, *RIGHT*, POSE WITH 2003 DRAFT PICKS KYLE BOLLER AND TERRELL SUGGS.

re-signed with his old team, Denver.

Because of the departures, the Ravens had 19 first-year players on their roster in 2002. The lack of experience was evident in a 7–9 season. Baltimore did have a veteran at quarterback in Jeff Blake. The former Cincinnati Bengal and New Orleans Saint signed with the Ravens in the offseason. He threw for 13 touchdowns with 11 interceptions.

The Ravens began the 2003 season with another new quarterback—rookie Kyle Boller. Baltimore selected Boller with the nineteenth pick in the NFL Draft. Boller had been a star

TRYING TO RECAPTURE GLORY **29**

> ### JONATHAN OGDEN
> Through the Ravens' ups and downs, offensive tackle Jonathan Ogden was consistently excellent. Baltimore selected Ogden, a former standout at the University of California, Los Angeles (UCLA), with the first draft choice in team history, fourth overall in 1996. Ogden made his first Pro Bowl after the 1997 season, his second year in the NFL. He would make the Pro Bowl every season through 2007 and be chosen as an All-Pro nine times. The 6-foot-9, 340-pound Ogden excelled at pass blocking and run blocking. Ogden retired after the 2007 season.

at the University of California, Berkeley. He was one of two first-round selections for the Ravens in 2003. The team also drafted linebacker Terrell Suggs with the tenth overall choice. He was an All-American at Arizona State University.

Boller started nine games in 2003. Baltimore finished 5–4 in them. When Boller went down with a season-ending thigh injury in November, backup Anthony Wright stepped in to play. He led the team to five victories in the final six games. The Ravens finished 10–6 and won the AFC North title. It was the first division championship in team history. The AFC North was created in 2002 when the NFL went from six divisions to eight. The other teams in the AFC North were Cincinnati, Cleveland, and Pittsburgh.

There were plenty of reasons for Baltimore's success in 2003. Suggs finished with 12 sacks and was named the NFL Defensive Rookie of the Year. Of course, the Ravens still had star linebacker Ray Lewis. He finished with 121 solo tackles and six interceptions. He was chosen as the NFL Defensive Player of the Year for the second time. Second-year safety Ed Reed had seven interceptions and was selected as an All-Pro. Then

THROUGH 2009, JAMAL LEWIS'S 2,066 RUSHING YARDS FOR BALTIMORE IN 2003 WERE THE SECOND MOST IN A SEASON IN NFL HISTORY.

there was running back Jamal Lewis. He had a highly successful season. He rushed for 2,066 yards and 14 touchdowns. He set an NFL record with 295 rushing yards in Baltimore's 33–13 home win over Cleveland in the second week. Third-year tight end Todd Heap had 57 catches, leading the team in receptions for the second straight year.

The Ravens played host to the Tennessee Titans in the wild-card round of the playoffs on January 3, 2004. Gary Anderson made a 46-yard field goal with 29 seconds remaining to lift Tennessee to a 20–17 victory. Jamal Lewis was held to 35 rushing yards.

It was a disappointing end to the season. The offseason was

THE RAVENS' ED REED RUNS WITH THE BALL IN 2004. THE SAFETY DEVELOPED A KNACK FOR MAKING BIG PLAYS IN THE SECONDARY AND ON SPECIAL TEAMS.

STEVE BISCIOTTI

On April 9, 2004, Steve Bisciotti purchased complete ownership of the Ravens. He previously had bought 49 percent of the team from owner Art Modell in 2000. When Bisciotti took over as the principal owner, it marked the end of 44 years of NFL ownership for Modell with the Cleveland Browns and Ravens. Bisciotti had built his fortune by starting a firm that provides temporary workers to other companies in fields such as engineering and computer programming.

also difficult. Jamal Lewis faced federal drug trafficking charges. He would plead guilty and spend time in jail, but not until after the 2004 season. The NFL suspended him for two games in 2004. He ran for 1,006 yards despite playing in just 12 games. But the offense struggled. Boller threw for just 13 touchdowns. The defense, led by Ray Lewis,

Reed, and star newcomer Deion Sanders at cornerback, was still a strength. Reed had nine interceptions and was NFL Defensive Player of the Year. But the team went 9–7 and did not make the postseason.

Jamal Lewis served a four-month prison sentence before the 2005 season and had knee surgery. He rushed for 906 yards but averaged just 3.4 yards per carry. Boller, meanwhile, injured a toe in the regular-season opener against Indianapolis. He would not return until more than halfway through the season. Baltimore also dealt with injuries to Ray Lewis and Reed. The Ravens went 6–10.

Baltimore would change direction again at quarterback before the 2006 season. It would turn out to be the Ravens' best move at that position since signing Dilfer.

ED REED

The Ravens chose safety Ed Reed in the first round, twenty-fourth overall, in the 2002 NFL Draft. Like linebacker Ray Lewis, Reed played at the University of Miami in Florida. Also like Lewis, Reed would become one of the top defensive players in the NFL.

Reed had five interceptions as a rookie with the Ravens in 2002. He made the Pro Bowl and was selected as an All-Pro every season from 2003 through 2009, except for 2005. That year, he played in just 10 games because of an ankle injury. He was selected as the NFL Defensive Player of the Year in 2004. Through 2009, Reed had seven interceptions or more in a season four times.

Reed broke his own league record when he returned an interception 107 yards for a touchdown in 2008. He intercepted the ball deep in the end zone and returned it all the way to the other end zone against the Philadelphia Eagles on November 23. His previous record was 106 yards.

CHAPTER 5

RETURN TO WINNING WAYS

The Ravens' defense had remained very strong in the seasons after the 2000 team's Super Bowl triumph. The problem was that the offense did not play well. In particular, the quarterback position was a concern.

In June 2006, Baltimore found the quarterback it was seeking. The Ravens traded a fourth-round pick in the 2007 NFL Draft to the Tennessee Titans for veteran Steve McNair. McNair had battled injuries. But McNair was known as a tough player. He would show that toughness with Baltimore in 2006, his twelfth season in the NFL.

McNair stepped in as the starting quarterback. Kyle Boller was his backup. The Ravens had improved their receiving corps before the previous season when they signed Derrick Mason, a former teammate of McNair's,

BALTIMORE QUARTERBACK STEVE MCNAIR RUNS AGAINST KANSAS CITY IN 2006. THE GRITTY MCNAIR HELPED THE RAVENS GO 13–3 THAT SEASON.

RETURN TO WINNING WAYS 35

COLTS DEFENSIVE TACKLE RAHEEM BROCK STUFFS RAVENS RUNNING BACK JAMAL LEWIS IN INDIANAPOLIS' 15–6 PLAYOFF WIN ON JANUARY 13, 2007.

away from the Titans. They had also drafted wide receiver Mark Clayton in the first round out of the University of Oklahoma. Mason, Clayton, and tight end Todd Heap formed a solid pass-catching trio.

Baltimore's stronger passing attack combined with the running of a healthier Jamal Lewis and a still-ferocious defense was a winning formula in 2006. McNair started all 16 games. He finished with 16 touchdown passes against 12 interceptions. Heap, Mason, and Clayton each had at least 65 catches. Lewis rushed for 1,132 yards and nine touchdowns. Baltimore's defense ranked first in the NFL in yards and points allowed. All of these things resulted in a 13–3 record and an AFC North title.

The Ravens received a bye in the first round of the playoffs. In the next round, they would play host to the Indianapolis Colts in one of the most memorable games in Ravens history. Fans in Baltimore were extremely excited about the matchup.

But Indianapolis was no pushover. The team went 12–4 in the regular season and had a star in Peyton Manning. He drew comparisons to another legendary quarterback in Colts history—Johnny Unitas.

It was Indianapolis' defense, though, not Manning, that led the team to victory. Adam Vinatieri kicked five field goals and the Colts kept the Ravens out of the end zone in a 15–6 win. Baltimore committed four turnovers. Indianapolis would go on to win the Super Bowl.

Injuries derailed the Ravens' 2007 campaign. McNair played in just six games. Baltimore finished 5–11. Owner Steve Bisciotti fired Billick the day after the season ended.

McNair and standout offensive tackle Jonathan Ogden

> **MATT STOVER**
>
> Kicker Matt Stover played for the Ravens from their first season, 1996, through 2008. Stover was a Cleveland Brown from 1991 to 1995, then moved with the team when it relocated to Baltimore and became the Ravens in 1996. In 2006, he made 28 of 30 field-goal tries for an accuracy of 93.3 percent, the best in the NFL that season. The Ravens decided not to sign Stover before the 2009 season. Stover, in turn, signed with Indianapolis. On February 7, 2010, he became the oldest player to participate in a Super Bowl, at the age of 42 years, 11 days. He made a 38-yard field goal in the Colts' 31–17 loss to the New Orleans Saints.

> ### STEVE MCNAIR
> On April 17, 2008, Ravens quarterback Steve McNair retired after a 13-year career in the NFL. McNair starred at tiny Alcorn State University in Mississippi. He then played with the Houston/Tennessee franchise from 1995 through 2005 before joining Baltimore. He only played 22 games with the Ravens over two seasons. But he anchored the 13-win campaign in 2006. McNair passed for 174 touchdowns with just 119 interceptions in his career. He also rushed for 37 touchdowns. Tragically, McNair died in July 2009 when he was the victim of a homicide in Nashville, Tennessee.

announced their retirements after the 2007 season. Bisciotti, meanwhile, hired John Harbaugh to be the third coach in Ravens history. Harbaugh had been the defensive backs coach with the Philadelphia Eagles.

The Ravens used their first draft choice in 2008, the eighteenth pick overall, on quarterback Joe Flacco. Some questioned whether Flacco, who played at the University of Delaware, could make a successful jump to the NFL. Delaware did not compete against the top level of competition in the college ranks.

It was a new era for the Ravens in 2008. They were being led by a rookie coach and a rookie quarterback. Flacco was the starter right away.

Flacco was very calm and cool for a rookie. He started all 16 games and played well. He finished with 14 touchdown passes and 12 interceptions. Mason had 80 catches for 1,037 yards. The Ravens' defense was back to dominating. Safety Ed Reed and linebacker Ray Lewis led the way. Reed tied a career high with nine interceptions.

Baltimore finished 11–5, one game behind Pittsburgh in the AFC North. The Ravens earned a wild-card playoff berth.

RAVENS OWNER STEVE BISCIOTTI, *LEFT*, AND COACH JOHN HARBAUGH APPEAR AT A NEWS CONFERENCE AFTER HARBAUGH WAS HIRED IN JANUARY 2008.

The Ravens routed the Dolphins 27–9 in Miami in the first round of the playoffs. Reed had two interceptions, returning one of them 64 yards for a touchdown. In the next round, Baltimore edged host Tennessee 13–10.

The Ravens advanced to the AFC Championship Game to face the Steelers in

JOHN HARBAUGH

Ravens coach John Harbaugh comes from a football family. His father, Jack, was a high school and college coach for 41 years. John's brother Jim played quarterback for 14 seasons in the NFL, including in 1998 with the Ravens, and then got into coaching. He became Stanford University's coach before the 2007 season. John had been a college assistant before the Philadelphia Eagles hired him in 1998. He served as the special teams coordinator and then defensive backs coach for the Eagles.

MICHAEL OHER

With its first-round selection, twenty-third overall, in the 2009 NFL Draft, Baltimore chose offensive tackle Michael Oher.

Oher started in all 16 games as a rookie with the Ravens and got his career off to a promising start. That was remarkable considering the circumstances in which Oher grew up in Memphis, Tennessee. He was one of 12 children. His mother was addicted to drugs, and he lived in foster homes and was homeless at times. He received a break when he was admitted to the private Briarcrest Christian School in high school. He was adopted by a family that had children at the school. These things changed Oher's life. He went on to play football at the University of Mississippi.

Oher's life is one of the subjects of Michael Lewis's 2006 book *The Blind Side: Evolution of a Game* and the basis of the 2009 film *The Blind Side*, which received an Academy Award nomination for Best Picture.

Pittsburgh. The game was a slugfest. Pittsburgh won 23–14. Flacco threw three interceptions. Pittsburgh would go on to win the Super Bowl.

Baltimore carried over its success from 2008 into 2009. Flacco continued to play with a maturity beyond his years. Second-year running back Ray Rice emerged as a star. He rushed for 1,339 yards and made 78 receptions. Mason had another 1,000-yard season. Baltimore's defense remained a strength.

The Ravens finished 9–7 in 2009 and earned another wild-card playoff spot. Baltimore faced the host New England Patriots in the postseason's first round. Rice ran for 159 yards and two touchdowns as the Ravens rolled to a 33–14 win. Baltimore intercepted New England star quarterback Tom Brady three times.

BALTIMORE QUARTERBACK JOE FLACCO HANDS THE BALL OFF TO RUNNING BACK RAY RICE IN A 33–14 PLAYOFF WIN AT NEW ENGLAND IN JANUARY 2010.

The Ravens' season ended the next week with a 20–3 loss at Indianapolis. The Colts would go on to reach the Super Bowl but lose.

The decade began with the Ravens winning a Super Bowl. By the end of that span, the team was winning playoff games again and still featuring a strong, intimidating defense. But the team also had young offensive standouts in Flacco and Rice. A new star joined the team in March 2010 when the Ravens acquired Pro Bowl wide receiver Anquan Boldin from the Arizona Cardinals for two draft picks. With these players and a young, talented coach in Harbaugh leading the way, the team's future appeared to be very promising.

TIMELINE

| 1984 | The Baltimore Colts, who had one of the richest traditions in the NFL over more than 30 seasons, move in the early morning hours on March 29 to Indianapolis. |

| 1996 | On February 9, the NFL approves the relocation of the Cleveland Browns franchise to Baltimore. |

| 1996 | After a *Baltimore Sun* phone poll, the new Baltimore team's nickname is officially chosen as Ravens on March 29. |

| 1996 | On September 1, the Ravens play their first NFL game before a sellout crowd of 64,124 at Memorial Stadium. Baltimore defeats the Oakland Raiders 19–14. |

| 1998 | The Ravens make their debut in their new downtown Baltimore stadium, called Ravens Stadium at the time (later to be named M&T Bank Stadium), on September 6. Baltimore loses 20–13 to the Pittsburgh Steelers. |

| 1998 | The Ravens play host to the Indianapolis Colts on November 29, marking the old franchise's first game in Baltimore since 1983. The Ravens rally to win 38–31. |

| 1999 | On January 19, former Minnesota Vikings offensive coordinator Brian Billick is named the Ravens' second coach. He succeeds Ted Marchibroda, whose contract was not renewed. |

| 2001 | After beating Denver and Tennessee in the team's first two playoff contests, the Ravens defeat host Oakland 16–3 in the AFC Championship Game on January 14. |

 2001	The Ravens crush the New York Giants 34–7 in Super Bowl XXXV on January 28 in Tampa, Florida. Baltimore's defense caps a dominant season by preventing New York from scoring an offensive touchdown. Linebacker Ray Lewis is selected as the game's Most Valuable Player.
2003	Ravens running back Jamal Lewis sets an NFL single-game record with 295 rushing yards in Baltimore's 33–13 victory over visiting Cleveland on September 14.
 2007	After a team-best 13–3 regular season, the Ravens fall 15–6 to the visiting Colts on January 13 in the divisional round of the playoffs.
2007	On December 31, the Ravens dismiss Billick as coach the day after they completed a 5–11 season.
 2008	On January 19, the Ravens hire John Harbaugh to replace Billick as coach. Harbaugh had been the defensive backs coach with the Philadelphia Eagles.
2008	Baltimore selects University of Delaware quarterback Joe Flacco with the team's first-round selection, eighteenth overall, in the NFL Draft on April 26.
 2009	In January, Flacco helps lead the Ravens to road victories over the Miami Dolphins and Tennessee Titans in the playoffs. He becomes the first NFL rookie quarterback to start and win two postseason games. Baltimore loses at Pittsburgh in the AFC title game.
 2010	On January 10, the Ravens rout the host New England Patriots 33–14 in a wild-card playoff game. Ray Rice runs for 159 yards and two touchdowns. The next week, Baltimore loses at Indianapolis in the divisional round.

QUICK STATS

FRANCHISE HISTORY
1996–

SUPER BOWLS
(wins in bold)
2000 (XXXV)

AFC CHAMPIONSHIP GAMES
2000, 2008

DIVISION CHAMPIONSHIPS
2003, 2006

KEY PLAYERS
(position, seasons with team)

Peter Boulware (LB, 1997–2005)
Joe Flacco (QB, 2008–)
Todd Heap (TE, 2001–)
Jamal Lewis (RB; 2000, 2002–06)
Ray Lewis (LB, 1996–)
Derrick Mason (WR, 2005–)
Chris McAlister (CB, 1999–2008)
Steve McNair (QB, 2006–07)
Jonathan Ogden (OT, 1996–2007)
Ed Reed (S, 2002–)
Ray Rice (RB, 2008–)
Matt Stover (K, 1996–2008)
Terrell Suggs (LB, 2003–)
Rod Woodson (DB, 1998–2001)

KEY COACHES
Brian Billick (1999–2007):
    80–64–0; 5–3 (playoffs)
John Harbaugh (2007–):
    20–12–0; 3–2 (playoffs)

HOME FIELDS
M&T Bank Stadium (1998–)
    Also known as Ravens Stadium
    in 1998 and 2002 and PSINet
    Stadium 1999–2001
Memorial Stadium (1996–97)

* All statistics through 2009 season

QUOTES AND ANECDOTES

"I've got no problem playing second fiddle to our defense. We do things that make us better. We were second in the league in time of possession. We have a ton of explosive plays. We were best in the league in turnover ratio. My teammates carried me. I don't know how good I am, but I'm the best quarterback for this team right now."
—Quarterback Trent Dilfer, talking during the 2000 playoffs about the offense's contributions to the defense-oriented Ravens' success that season

When the Ravens won Super Bowl XXXV in January 2001, they became the third team in NFL history to win a Super Bowl after making the playoffs as a wild-card team. The 1980 Oakland Raiders and 1997 Denver Broncos also accomplished the feat. Later, the 2005 Pittsburgh Steelers and 2007 New York Giants did the same.

Ravens star safety Ed Reed, who has also been a standout on special teams, became the first player in NFL history to score a touchdown on an interception return, a blocked punt, a punt return, and a fumble return. Through 2009, he had scored 12 touchdowns in his career—six on interceptions, three on blocked punts, two on fumble returns, and one on a punt return.

After quarterback Steve McNair announced his retirement in 2008, no player took it harder than linebacker Ray Lewis. Lewis said, "There is no greater warrior or player with a bigger heart than Steve McNair. He came into this game and gave it everything he had. He now can walk away with his head held high."

GLOSSARY

berth
A place, spot, or position, such as in the NFL playoffs.

bye
The position of a team or person in a tournament that advances to the next round without playing.

contract
A binding agreement about, for example, years of commitment by a football player in exchange for a given salary.

draft
A system used by professional sports leagues to select new players in order to spread incoming talent among all teams.

franchise
An entire sports organization, including the players, coaches, and staff.

hall of fame
A place built to honor noteworthy achievements by athletes in their respective sports.

legendary
Well known and admired over a long period.

mediocre
Neither good nor bad.

postseason
Games played in the playoffs by the top teams after the regular-season schedule has been completed.

Pro Bowl
A game after the regular season in which the top players from the AFC play against the top players from the NFC.

rookie
A first-year professional athlete.

sack
Term used when a defensive player tackles the quarterback behind the line of scrimmage.

stingy
In football, a defense that is difficult to score or move the ball against.

FOR MORE INFORMATION

Further Reading

Billick, Brian, and Michael MacCambridge. *More than a Game: The Glorious Present and Uncertain Future of the NFL.* New York: Scribner, 2009.

Lewis, Michael. *The Blind Side: Evolution of a Game (movie tie-in edition).* New York: W. W. Norton & Company, 2009.

Matte, Tom, and Jeff Seidel. *Tom Matte's Tales from the Baltimore Ravens Sideline.* Champaign, IL: Sports Publishing LLC, 2004.

Web Links

To learn more about the Baltimore Ravens, visit ABDO Publishing Company online at **www.abdopublishing.com**. Web sites about the Ravens are featured on our Book Links page. These links are routinely monitored and updated to provide the most current information available.

Places to Visit

M&T Bank Stadium
1101 Russel Street
Baltimore, MD 21230
410-261-7283
www.baltimoreravens.com/Gameday/
 MT_Bank_Stadium.aspx
This stadium, completed in 1998 at an estimated cost of $220 million, is where the Ravens play all their home games.

Pro Football Hall of Fame
2121 George Halas Drive Northwest
Canton, OH 44708
330-456-8207
www.profootballhof.com
This hall of fame and museum highlights the greatest players and moments in the history of the National Football League. As of 2010, one player affiliated with the Ravens—defensive back Rod Woodson—had been enshrined.

Ravens Training Camp
McDaniel College
451 WMC Drive
Westminster, MD 21158
410-840-5000
The Ravens have held summer training camp at McDaniel College since their first year in existence, 1996.

INDEX

Adams, Sam, 6, 25, 28
Alexander, Derrick, 20
Anderson, Gary, 31

Banks, Tony, 7, 9, 24, 25
Billick, Brian (coach), 7, 24, 37
Bisciotti, Steve (owner), 32, 37, 38
Blake, Jeff, 29
Boldin, Anquan, 41
Boller, Kyle, 29, 30, 32, 33, 35
Boulware, Peter, 6, 21, 25 28
Burnett, Rob, 6, 28
Byner, Earnest, 19

Clayton, Mark, 36

Dilfer, Trent, 6, 7, 9, 10, 25, 27, 28, 33

Flacco, Joe, 38, 40, 41

Grbac, Elvis, 27, 28

Harbaugh, Jim, 22, 24, 39
Harbaugh, John (coach), 38, 39, 41
Harris, Corey, 23
Heap, Todd, 31, 36
Herring, Kim, 6

Ismail, Qadry, 8, 25

Jackson, Michael, 20
Johnson, Patrick, 23

Lewis, Jamal, 8–10, 25, 28, 31–33, 36
Lewis, Jermaine, 8, 9
Lewis, Marvin (assistant coach), 6
Lewis, Ray, 6, 10, 17, 21, 25, 28, 30, 32, 33, 38

M&T Bank Stadium, 14, 22
Marchibroda, Ted (coach), 16, 23
Mason, Derrick, 35, 36, 38, 40
McAlister, Chris, 7, 25, 28
McCrary, Michael, 6, 25
McNair, Steve, 35–38
Memorial Stadium, 15, 17, 19, 20
Modell, Art (owner), 14, 16, 17, 32

Newsome, Ozzie (general manager), 16, 28

Ogden, Jonathan, 17, 28, 30, 37
Oher, Michael, 40

PSINet Stadium, 22

Ravens Stadium, 21, 22
Reed, Ed, 28, 30, 33, 38, 39
Rice, Ray, 40, 41

Sanders, Deion, 33
Sharpe, Shannon, 6, 8, 28
Sharper, Jamie, 6
Siragusa, Tony, 6, 25
Starks, Duane, 7, 9, 28
Stokley, Brandon, 9
Stover, Matt, 8, 9, 19, 37
Suggs, Terrell, 30
Super Bowl XXXV, 5–8, 10, 11, 25, 27, 35

Testaverde, Vinny, 19, 20, 22

Unitas, Johnny, 13, 14, 37

Woodson, Rod, 6, 23, 25, 28

About the Author

Andy Jasner is a freelance writer based in the Philadelphia, Pennsylvania, area. Jasner has covered the National Football League, National Basketball Association, National Hockey League, and Major League Baseball as well as other professional, college, and high school sporting events since graduating from Syracuse University in 1991. He lives with his wife and two daughters.